Presented to

_____

_____

Stories for the Teacher's Heart

COMPILED *by* ALICE GRAY
ARTWORK *by* SUSAN WINGET

Multnomah Gifts™

Multnomah®Publishers *Sisters, Oregon*

Stories for the Teacher's Heart

© 2002 by Multnomah Publishers, Inc.
published by Multnomah Publishers, Inc.
P.O. Box 1720, Sisters, Oregon 97759

ISBN 1-57673-918-X

Other books in the Stories for the Heart Collection:
Stories for the Grad's Heart
Stories for A Cheerful Heart

Artwork © 2002 by Susan Winget

Designed by Koechel Peterson & Associates, Minneapolis, Minnesota

Printed in China

02 03 04 05 06 07 08 — 10 9 8 7 6 5 4 3 2 1 0

www.multnomahgifts.com

TABLE OF CONTENTS

The Hand

AUTHOR UNKNOWN

A Thanksgiving Day editorial in the newspaper told of a schoolteacher who asked her first-graders to draw a picture of something they were thankful for. She thought of how little these children from poor neighborhoods actually had to be thankful for. But she knew that most of them would draw pictures of turkeys on tables with food. The teacher was taken aback with the picture Douglas handed in…a simple childishly drawn hand.

But whose hand? This class was captivated by the abstract image. "I think it must be the hand of God that brings us food," said one child. "A farmer," said another, "because he grows the turkeys." Finally when the others were back at work the teacher bent over Douglas's desk and asked whose hand it was. "It's your hand, Teacher," he mumbled.

She recalled that frequently at recess she had taken Douglas, a scrubby forlorn child, by the hand. She often did that with the children. But it meant so much to Douglas.

Perhaps this was everyone's Thanksgiving, not for the material things given to us but for the chance, in whatever small way, to give to others.

The true aim of every tea
is not to impart his
own opinion... but to
kindle minds.

The Student's Mite

DAVID R. COLLINS

The situation seemed hopeless.

From the first day he entered my seventh-grade classroom, Willard P. Franklin had existed in his own world, shutting out his classmates and me, his teacher. My attempts at establishing a friendly relationship were met with complete indifference. Even a "Good morning, Willard" received only an inaudible grunt. His classmates fared no better. Willard was strictly a loner, finding no desire or need to lower the barrier of silence he had erected. His clothes were clean—but definitely not on the cutting edge of style. He could have been a trend setter because his outfits possessed a "hand-me-down" look before such a look was in. Shortly after the Thanksgiving holidays, we received an announcement regarding the annual Christmas collection.

"Christmas is a season of giving," I told my students. "There are a few students in the school who might not have a happy holiday season. By contributing to our Christmas collection, you will help to buy food, clothing and toys for these needy people. You may bring your money tomorrow."

When I called for the contributions the next day, I discovered everyone had forgotten—everyone except Willard P. Franklin. The boy dug deep into his pants pockets as he strolled up to my desk. Carefully he dropped a nickel into the small container.

"I don't need no milk for lunch," he mumbled. For a moment, just a moment, he smiled. I watched him turn and walk back to his desk.

That night, after school, I took our meager contribution—one lone nickel—to the school principal. I couldn't help telling him the giver's identity and sharing with him the incident.

"I may be wrong, but I believe Willard may be ready to

become a part of the world around him," I told the principal.

"Yes, I believe it sounds hopeful," he nodded. "And I have a hunch we might profit from him letting us share a bit of his world. I just received a list of the poor families of our school who most need help through the Christmas collection. Here, look at it."

And as I gazed down to read, I discovered Willard P. Franklin and his family were the top names on the list.

Teachings of youth…make impressions on the mind and heart that are to last forever. The highest function of the teacher consists not so much in imparting knowledge, as in stimulating the pupil in its love and pursuit.

HENRI FREDERIC AMIEL

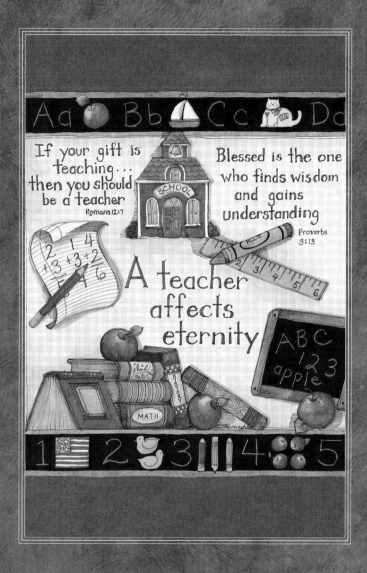

Hope Which Springs Eternal

GUY RICE DOUD

Mr. Card was my sixth-grade teacher and my first male teacher. When I walked into class that first day, I was surprised to see a man in the room. I wondered if this man was a new janitor, but I guessed not because he had on dress slacks, a white shirt and a tie. I examined him. He looked too young to be a teacher.

By the time I had reached sixth grade, I was quite discouraged about school and life. I had learned I wasn't one of the brightest kids in class. I was horrible at math. My artwork had been left off the bulletin board. The teacher was always telling me that I had to keep a clean desk, and I just couldn't figure how Mary, who sat next to me, could keep her desk so organized. I sang too loud. No one ever picked me first while choosing teams for kickball. I was never the captain, and I had concluded I would never be the captain or one of the popular kids.

No one deliberately set out to teach me these things, and no one, except a few classmates who made fun of my size, ever purposely meant to hurt me. But I had come to believe I wasn't very good.

I was worried when I realized Mr. Card was going to be my teacher. Men aren't as nice as women, you know. Men are hard and don't have the sympathy women do. At least that's what I thought at the time. And I felt I needed someone who would have sympathy for me; Mr. Card didn't look like he would.

I studied him some more. He walked over to me, held out his hand and said, "Hi, I'm Mr. Card. Norm Card. I'm going to be your teacher."

I had never had a teacher shake my hand before, but I extended my hand and obliged.

"What's your name?" he asked.

"Guy Doud."

"Oh, I've heard about you."

Oh no, I thought. *You've heard that I'm no good at math*

or art, and that I don't like SRA boxes. You know I sing too loud and have a messy desk. You probably know about my mom and dad and that we're not very rich and we've never been to Disneyland or any place like that....

But I've never found out what Mr. Card knew, and I've never asked him, because he treated me like somebody special. I guess he treated all the kids that way, but what mattered to me was the way he treated me, and it felt good.

Mr. Card was a first-year teacher, right out of college. He did things with us I didn't think teachers were allowed to do. He played with us at recess. He ran around and yelled like a big kid.

We had graduated from kickball to touch football, and Mr. Card was always on one of our teams. He was the quarterback. He didn't let us pick the teams. He divided us up, and he took turns playing for both teams.

One day when he was on my team he said, "Guy, I want you to go out for the pass. Go down the left side.

Cut across. When you get to the middle, I'll hit you with the pass."

It gave me such confidence to know that Mr. Card trusted me enough to throw to me. I had come to believe that my role in football was to block, but Mr. Card was giving me my chance to be a receiver.

I lined up as he called the signals. I felt my heart beating in my head. I wanted to catch this ball. I wanted to prove that not just fast, skinny kids could be receivers. I could catch it, too.

The ball was centered. I was off like a slow train, but I was bound and determined to reach my destination.

Mr. Card was elusive in the backfield. Sometimes he would run around back there for what seemed like twenty minutes as we tried to touch him. Just when you thought you had him, he would jump out of the way. This was good as far as I was concerned, because as he was eluding would-be tacklers, I was starting my cut across the center of the playing field.

No one was paying much attention to me. My being a receiver had never been a part of anyone's game plan. It took everyone by surprise when Mr. Card unloaded the football and threw a strike right to me.

He threw it so hard that if one of the skinny kids had been catching the ball, it would have carried him an extra three yards. But it went through my hands, hit my belly, and was starting to bounce away when I pulled it in, smothering it in the folds of my stomach.

I caught it! I was so excited I forgot to run, and Marty quickly touched me. I've since wished we had been playing tackle football because I was so proud after catching that ball that I think I could have carried the entire sixth-grade class into the end zone.

I liked Mr. Card. He came by my desk to check my work, and as he looked it over, he rested his hand on my shoulder. His hand, although extremely heavy and causing me a great deal of anxiety, said, *I like you, Guy. You're okay.*

Sometimes I would raise my hand, kind of hoping

that maybe Mr. Card would come by my desk. Maybe his hand would need a place to rest for a moment, and he would use my shoulder.

I worked hard for him, and he told me I was a good worker. I came to believe that maybe doing your best and working hard was even more important than being really smart and getting your artwork up on the bulletin board.

The last week of class Mr. Card handed out awards. It was a full-blown ceremony. He seemed to find something to give everyone. He even gave an award for the person who had to ride the farthest on the bus every day. He got down to the two last awards and said he thought these awards were the two most important of all, for they would go to the hardest working girl and the hardest working boy.

I wondered who would win those awards. I surveyed the room. I figured either Mary or Linda would win for the girls, and I bet probably Sam or Danny would win for the boys.

"The award for the hardest working boy in Mr. Card's sixth-grade class goes to Guy Doud."

I heard him say it, but I didn't believe it.

"Guy, come on up and get your award."

I rose from my desk. I was the only one with a steel desk. Mr. Hill had gone to the junior high and brought back a steel desk for me after I had broken my wooden one. I had rocked backward in it, and one of the legs had broken.

"Hardest Working Boy in Mr. Card's Sixth-Grade Class"—that's what the certificate said. Just a plain piece of mimeographed paper; but it couldn't have meant more to me if it had been a gold statue.

My mom felt the same way, because she left it on the door of the refrigerator, until I took it down about three weeks into seventh grade.

A teacher affects eternity;

He can never tell where his influence stops.

HENRY BROOKS ADAMS

A Student's Plea

MELISSA ANN BROECKELMAN

Teach me to strive for success; challenge me
Let fantasy become reality;
Allow my well of knowledge to run deep
Develop this mind that I'll always keep;
Give me instructions and provide a means
To see that the path isn't as it seems;
Give me assurance and let me believe
That with persistence, my dreams I'll achieve;
I want to prove no goal is out of reach
Show me the right direction, I beseech;
Let me dissolve each mental boundary
So I can reach out and seize the victory;
Push me to extents far beyond extremes
Do this, and you'll help me attain my dreams.

Choosing Mary

DAN TAYLOR

When I was in the sixth grade I was an all-American. I was smart, athletic, witty, handsome and incredibly nice. Things went down hill fast in junior high, but for this one year at least, I had everything.

Of course I also had Miss Owens for an assistant teacher. She helped Mr. Jenkins, our regular teacher. She knew that even though I was smart and incredibly nice, there was still a thing or two I could work on.

One of the things you were expected to do in grade school was learn to dance. My parents may have had some reservations at first, but since this was square dancing, it was okay.

Every time we went to work on our dancing, we did this terrible thing. The boys would all line up at the door to our classroom. Then, one at a time, each boy would pick a girl to be his partner. The girls all sat at their desks. As

they were chosen, they left their desks and joined the snot-nosed kids who had honored them with their favor.

Believe me, the boys did not like doing this—at least I didn't. But think about being one of those girls. Think about waiting to get picked. Think about seeing who was going to get picked before you. Think about worrying that you'd get picked by someone you couldn't stand. Think about worrying whether you were going to get picked at all!

Think if you were Mary. Mary sat near the front of the classroom on the right side. She wasn't pretty. She wasn't real smart. She wasn't witty. She was nice, but that wasn't enough in those days. And Mary certainly wasn't athletic. In fact, she'd had polio or something when she was younger; one of her arms was drawn up, and she had a bad leg, and to finish it off, she was kind of heavy.

Here's where Miss Owens comes in. Miss Owens took me aside one day and said, "Dan, next time we have square dancing, I want you to choose Mary."

Well, she may as well have told me to fly to Mars. It was an idea that was so new and inconceivable that I could barely hold it in my head. You mean pick someone other than the best, the most pretty, the most popular, when my turn came? That seemed like breaking a law of nature or something.

And then Miss Owens did a rotten thing. She told me it was what a Christian should do. I knew immediately that I was doomed. I was doomed because I knew she was right. It was exactly the thing Jesus would have done. I was surprised, in fact, that I hadn't seen it on a Sunday school flannel board yet: "Jesus choosing the lame girl for the Yeshiva dance." It was bound to be somewhere in the Bible.

I agonized. Choosing Mary would go against all the coolness I had accumulated.

The day came when we were to square dance again. If God really loved me, I thought, He will make me last. Then picking Mary will cause no stir. I will have done the right thing, and it won't have cost me anything.

You can guess where I was instead. For whatever reason, Mr. Jenkins made me first in line. There I was, my heart pounding—now I knew how some of the girls must have felt.

The faces of the girls were turned toward me, some smiling. I looked at Mary and saw that she was half turned to the back of the room, her face staring down at her desk. Mr. Jenkins said, "Okay, Dan—choose your partner."

I remember feeling very far away. I heard my voice say, "I choose Mary."

Never has reluctant virtue been so rewarded. I still see her face undimmed in my memory. She lifted her head, and on her face, reddened with pleasure and surprise and embarrassment all at the same time, was the most genuine look of delight and even pride that I had ever seen, before or since. It was so pure that I had to look away because I knew I didn't deserve it.

Mary came and took my arm, as we had been instructed, and she walked beside me, bad leg and all, just like a princess.

Mary is my age. I never saw her after that year. I don't know what her life's been like or what she's doing. But I'd like to think she has a fond memory of at least one day in sixth grade. I know I do.

Don't judge by
appearance or height . . .
the Lord doesn't make
decisions the way you do.
People judge by outward
appearance but the Lord
looks at the heart.

1 SAMUEL 16:7, NLT

Giving and Receiving

BILLIE DAVIS

A public school teacher made clear to me the complex ideas of giving and receiving.

Evidently she noticed something about the way I held the book in reading class and arranged for an eye examination. She did not send me to a clinic; she took me to her own oculist, not as a charity case but as a friend. Indeed, I was so intrigued with the activity that I did not realize exactly what had happened until one day at school she gave me the glasses.

"I can't take them. I can't pay for them," I said, embarrassed by my family's poverty.

She told me a story: "When I was a child, a neighbor bought glasses for me. She said I should pay for them someday by getting glasses for some other little girl. So, you see, the glasses were paid for before you were born."

Then the teacher said the most welcome words that anyone had ever said to me: "Someday you will buy glasses for some other little girl."

She saw me as a giver. She made me responsible. She believed I might have something to offer to someone else. She accepted me as a member of the same world she lived in. I walked out of that room, clutching the glasses, not as a recipient of charity, but as a trusted courier.

May those whose holy task

is to guide impulsive youth,

Fail not to cherish in their souls

a reverence for truth;

For teachings which the

lips impart, must have

their source within the heart.

CHARLOTTE FORTEN GRIMKE

A Gift I'll Never Forget

LINDA DEMERS HUMMEL

He entered my life twenty years ago, leaning against the doorjamb of Room 202, where I taught fifth grade. He wore sneakers three sizes too large and checkered pants ripped at the knees.

Daniel, as I'll call him, though that was not his real name, made this undistinguished entrance in the school of a quaint lakeside village known for its old money, white colonial homes, and brass mailboxes. He told me his last school had been in a neighboring county. "We were pickin' fruit," he said matter-of-factly.

I suspected this friendly, scruffy, smiling boy from a migrant family had no idea he had been thrown into a den of fifth-grade lions who had never before seen torn pants. If he noticed snickering, he didn't let on. There was no chip on his shoulder.

Twenty-five children eyed Daniel suspiciously until

the kickball game that afternoon. Then he led off the first inning with a home run. With it came a bit of respect from the wardrobe critics of Room 202.

Next was Charles's turn. Charles was the least athletic, most overweight child in the history of fifth grade. After his second strike, amid the rolled eyes and groans of the class, Daniel edged up and spoke quietly to Charles's dejected back. "Forget them, kid. You can do it."

Charles warmed, smiled, stood taller and promptly struck out anyway. But at that precise moment, defying the social order of this jungle he had entered, Daniel had gently begun to change things—and us.

By autumn's end, we had all gravitated toward him. He taught us all kinds of lessons. How to call a wild turkey. How to tell whether fruit is ripe before that first bite. How to treat others, even Charles. Especially Charles. He never did use our names, calling me "Miss" and the students "kid."

The day before Christmas vacation, the students always brought gifts for the teacher. It was a ritual—opening each

department-store box, surveying the expensive perfume or scarf or leather wallet, and thanking the child.

That afternoon, Daniel walked to my desk and bent close to my ear. "Our packing boxes came out last night," he said without emotion. "We're leavin' tomorrow."

As I grasped the news, my eyes filled with tears. He countered the awkward silence by telling me about the move. Then, as I regained my composure, he pulled a gray rock from his pocket. Deliberately and with great style, he pushed it gently across my desk.

I sensed that this was something remarkable, but all my practice with perfume and silk had left me pitifully unprepared to respond. "It's for you," he said, fixing his eyes on mine. "I polished it up special."

I've never forgotten that moment.

Years have passed since then. Each Christmas my daughter asks me to tell this story. It always begins after she has picked up the small polished rock that sits on my desk and nestles herself in my lap. The first words of the story

never vary. "The last time I ever saw Daniel, he gave me this rock as a gift and told me about his boxes. That was a long time ago, even before you were born.

"He's a grown-up now," I finish. Together we wonder where he is and what he has become.

"Someone good I bet," my daughter says. Then she adds, "Do the end of the story."

I know what she wants to hear—the lesson of love and caring learned by a teacher from a boy with nothing—and everything—to give. A boy who lived out of boxes. I touch the rock, remembering.

"Hi, kid," I say softly. "This is Miss. I hope you no longer need the packing boxes. And Merry Christmas, wherever you are."

Thoroughly to teach another

is the best way to learn for yourself.

TYRON EDWARDS

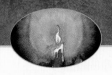

Lord,

I renounce my desire for human praise,

For the approval of my peers,

The need for public recognition.

I deliberately put these aside today,

Content to hear you whisper,

"Well done, my faithful servant."

Amen

To Whom It May Concern

INA HUGHS

*W*ouldn't it be nice if a mom could send her child out into the world with a list of instructions and a guarantee? The day they set out for kindergarten, all slicked up in a new outfit and carrying shiny new lunch boxes, if we mothers who smile and sniff back at the bus stop had our "druthers," we'd send along a letter that goes something like this:

> *To Whom It May Concern, and I Sure Hope It Does:*
>
> *This is a very special little five-year-old girl. She is especially special to her father, who is still mumbling incoherently about where all the time has gone.*
>
> *It seems like only yesterday when she spent her mornings flopping around in my shoes and watching Captain Kangaroo. However, if you know a few*

important things about her, I am sure she will love school as much as I did a hundred years ago.

Whenever she gets hurt or upset, she gets a stomachache. The best remedy is to put her on your lap and kiss her three times—on the cheek, neck, and forehead. Just a little family ritual perhaps you should know about. She likes to be called Snicklefritz, her daddy's pet name for her, which might come in handy if she gets homesick.

As for lunch, she doesn't like spinach, squash, asparagus, cooked carrots, yams (only sweet potatoes with marshmallows), beets, veal, or potato salad. She likes hot dogs (no mustard), hamburgers (with mayonnaise), soup (Campbell's Chicken & Stars), pizza (plain), and peanut butter (not the generic kind and never crunchy). Please add a teaspoon of sugar to her milk or else she will make a horrible face and may spit it out.

Her lunch money will be in a little purse around her neck. She knows her quarters from her nickels, but

dimes give her a fit. Just remind her a dime is the thing she swallowed once. If she ever should lose her money, please don't let her go hungry. We have MasterCard and Visa.

She forgets sometimes that she needs to go to the bathroom, but you can usually tell by the way she stands. She doesn't like to wash her hands before lunch, so will you patiently remind her about ten times?

Should there ever be a thunderstorm during school, please hold her hand and make jokes about how the angels must be bowling in heaven. I know that's not very scientific, but it helps. You'll probably need to comb her hair every day after recess. Please use only covered rubber bands, and I'm sure you can tell that it looks better parted on the left.

She's very worried about carrying her own lunch tray without the food sliding off, and about finding my car after school. So, would you carry her tray for, say, the first six months? My car is a green Dodge, and there will be a dog waiting in it with me.

She has several special talents perhaps you should know about. For instance, she made up a cute little song about a bumble bee. If you ever could use it, I am sure her father would be delighted to come do the background buzzing. She can make French toast in her Easy-Bake oven, get to fifteen doing the lemon twist, and recently wrote a poem about "Giggley, the Wiggley Worm," which might be nice for the school paper.

If you will remember these few things about our precious angel, I am sure she will be your favorite student, destined to fame in the Red Robin Reading Group, the Talent Development Program, the Safety Patrol and, eventually, Phi Beta Kappa.

Should you need me, don't hesitate to call: 373-0689 (home); 332-5123 (office); 375-3969 (next door); 352-8197 (her dad's office); 382-1763 (the grocery store where I shop, just in case); 387-5211 (where Dad eats lunch); or 374-2221 (police).

I'll be happy to come sit in the desk with her, if you ever need me.

P.S. Please don't make her grow up too fast. We like her just the way she is!

The most potent of all indirect influences
in the development of our citizenry
is the influence of a good teacher.

ARMOND J. GERSON

The Lesson
TERESA OLIVE

Occasionally, a teacher comes along who can lift students out of the dreary routine of their workbook exercises and tests—a teacher who views education as an exciting journey and a lifelong process of discovery.

In my sophomore year of high school, I was blessed with such a teacher. Her name was Mrs. Roberts, though some of the seniors still slipped and called her by her maiden name.

Her recent marriage had surprised most of us, since we "mature" high schoolers considered anyone over forty too ancient for such things as romance. However, her newly acquired habit of humming in the halls indicated that she had adjusted quite well to married life. In fact, some of the seniors grumbled that we sophomores had it easy compared to what her classes had been like before she hummed in the halls.

It isn't that she was mean; it's just that she seemed to expect the impossible. A lot of us lacked in ability to write a decent paragraph, and Mrs. Roberts intended to change that state of affairs.

We dissected *Newsweek* and *Time* articles as if they were frogs in biology class. But our daily assignments were still returned with more red ink than black—most of it used to cross out words, phrases, even entire paragraphs. "Unnecessary" and "overly descriptive" words were Mrs. Roberts's enemies, and she attacked them ruthlessly.

In spite of our complaints, though, we really liked Mrs. Roberts. She didn't teach English as a way to make a living. She taught it because she was committed to it—and to us. She was determined to push us out of our cozy nest of complacent ignorance, knowing we were meant to fly.

Then one day she was absent. The whispered news spread across the room: Mrs. Roberts's husband had been killed in a car accident by a drunk driver who had veered into his lane, hitting him head on.

Five days later, when Mrs. Roberts came back, she didn't hum as she came down the hall, but otherwise she acted as if nothing unusual had happened.

"Turn to page 97," she ordered in her usual brisk voice. The sound of rustling pages seemed amplified by the awkward silence. Finally, two girls in the front row stepped up to her desk and one of them stammered, "Mrs. Roberts, we—we're really sorry about what happened."

Her face contorted, Mrs. Roberts failed in her struggle for control and dropped her head on her desk, her shoulders heaving. The two girls gently patted her back as the rest of us watched helplessly.

When she at last regained some composure, she wiped off her glasses, looked at us and said, "I'm sorry. I thought I could handle this on my own, but I see now that I can't. You'll just have to bear with me for a while."

The tension was dissolved in a chorus of reassuring voices. "That's okay, Mrs. Roberts. Don't worry about us."

"All right," she said, putting back her glasses along with her best nononsense voice. "Let's get back to dangling participles."

That was the day that woke most of us to the strange notion that grown-ups could be vulnerable, too. Students often gathered around Mrs. Roberts between classes. Sometimes she would show them her husband's picture, which she kept in a locket around her neck. Tears became less frequent, but when they did slip out, someone would murmur an encouraging word.

Mrs. Roberts was a rare teacher. She taught us to be better writers. Even now, when I write, I can hear her crisp voice: "If it isn't necessary, cross it out." More important, though, she taught us that our need for each other is not our weakness, but rather our strength. After all, when something is crossed out, that which remains means more than ever.

Teachers should be held in the highest honor.
They are the allies of legislators;
they have agency in the prevention of crime;
they aid in regulating the atmosphere,
whose incessant action and pressure
cause the life-blood to circulate,
and to return pure and healthful
to the heart of the nation.

LYDIA SIGOURNEY, 1791–1865

You Can Do It!

RICKY BYRDSONG

WITH DAVE AND NETA JACKSON

I remember it like it was yesterday. Tenth grade, Frederick Douglass High School in Atlanta. Tall and gangly, I was pushing my way through the crowded hallway. All of a sudden a big, booming voice pealed like a thunderclap behind me, "Hey, son!"

It was Coach William Lester. He was a big, barrel-chested man, six feet four inches. Besides being the junior varsity basketball coach, he also had a reputation as the school disciplinarian, so the first thing I thought was, *Uh-oh, somebody's in trouble.* He fixed me with his piercing eyes and bellowed, "Yeah, you, son!"

Weak-kneed, I started walking toward him. *Oh my, what had I done?* I stopped in front of him, all six feet five inches of me trembling in my shoes. "Son!" he said, looking me up and down. "You're too big to be walking these

halls and not playing basketball. I'll see you in the gym at 3:30—today."

"But, Coach!" I sputtered. "I've never played basketball. I don't have any basketball clothes or shoes."

"Son! Did you hear what I said? I'll see you at 3:30!" And he walked away.

So I went.

And from that day until now, there's no question in my mind that everything that has happened to me since—becoming a basketball player, then a coach, raising my three kids, writing a book—is a result of that day when coach called me out and said, "Hey, son! Yes, you!"

Up until that point, I hadn't been a troublemaker, but I was drifting. I had no idea what my goals were or where I was heading.

My mom, like so many parents—especially single, working parents—really didn't have time to think about those things. Her goals were pretty basic. "I don't want Ricky on drugs. I don't want him running with the wrong crowd."

Coach Lester helped me see something bigger out there. I remember when he told me, "You can get a college scholarship."

When I said, "But I don't know how. I don't have it," he said, "Yes, you do. I'm going to show you. I'm going to work with you. You can do it."

And he was right. I knew it the day I set foot on a college campus, scholarship in hand. He believed in me. I couldn't let him down.

Many times since the day I heard that big voice bellow, "Hey, son!" I've thought, *If only every kid had a Coach William Lester to believe in him, what a difference it would make.*

Encourage one another and build each other up.

1 THESSALONIANS 5:11, NIV

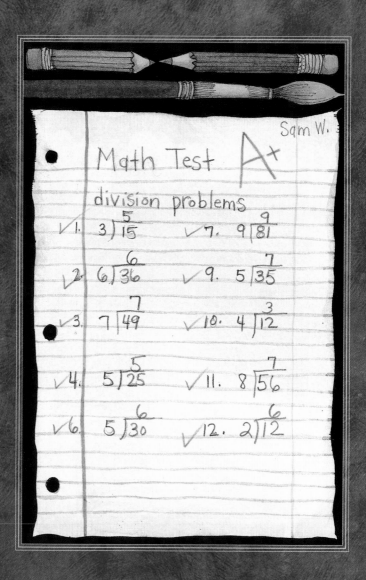

Mrs. Warren's Class

COLLEEN TOWNSEND EVANS

One of the great joys in life comes from watching a troubled person turn and go in a new—and better—direction. What causes such a thing to happen? A miracle? Sometimes. Forgiveness? Always!

Tom was a charming child, as most rascals are—but he was rebellious, a prankster, a rule breaker, a flaunter of authority. By the time he entered high school, his reputation had preceded him and he filled most of the teachers with dread. He took a special delight in disrupting classes and driving teachers to the limits of their patience. At home, he also was a problem. There were frequent confrontations between parents and child, each one seeking to prove he was more powerful than the other.

So many complaints were filed against Tom that the high school principal decided he would have to expel

him—unless a teacher named Mrs. Warren agreed to take him into her class. Mrs. Warren was an exceptionally capable English teacher, but she also was a loving, endlessly patient woman who seemed to have a way with problem students. Yes, Mrs. Warren said, she would find a place for him in her eleven o'clock English literature class, and also in her home room. She listened calmly as the principal read from a list of Tom's misdemeanors— a long list that had the principal shaking his head as he read. No, Mrs. Warren said, she wouldn't change her mind. She knew what she was getting into—she had heard about the boy.

When Tom was transferred to Mrs. Warren's class, he behaved as he always did upon meeting a new teacher. He slouched in his seat in the last row and glared at her, daring her—by his attitude—to do something about him. At first Mrs. Warren ignored him. Then, as the class began to discuss the reading assignment, Tom whispered a joke to the boy in front of him, making the boy laugh.

Mrs. Warren looked up. Then she closed her book, stood and placed another chair at the desk, next to hers.

"Tom, come up here and sit with me for a while," she said—not as a reprimand, but as a friend. It was an invitation she was offering, and her manner was so sweet that Tom couldn't refuse. He sat next to her as she went on with the lesson. "Tom is new to our class and hasn't had time to read the assignment, so if you'll bear with me, I'll read it aloud to him."

With Tom next to her, sharing her book, Mrs. Warren began to read from *A Tale of Two Cities*. She was a fine reader and captured Dickens' sense of drama magnificently. Tom, for all his determination to be an obstruction, found himself following the text, losing himself in the unfolding of a great story, sharing the excitement of it with a woman who really seemed to care about his interest in the book. That evening he startled his parents by sitting down without any prodding to do his homework—at least the assignment for Mrs. Warren's class.

That was only the beginning… Tom never missed a day of school after that first day in Mrs. Warren's class. Sometimes he cut other classes but never hers. He sat in the front row, participated in discussions, and seemed to enjoy reading aloud when he was called upon to do so. His appetite for reading suddenly became ravenous, and he asked Mrs. Warren to make up a list of books she thought he might enjoy in his free time. After school he stayed in the classroom when the other students went home and had long talks with Mrs. Warren about the things he had read and the ideas they stimulated.

Tom wasn't exactly an angel in other classes, but the effect of his behavior in Mrs. Warren's class began to rub off a little—for which the other teachers were most grateful.

Tom didn't finish high school. In his junior year, after an angry outburst at home, he defiantly joined the navy. He didn't even say good-bye to Mrs. Warren, who was very sad to see him leave school, because she thought she had failed in her attempt to reach him.

Seven years later, when Mrs. Warren was closing up her desk one afternoon before leaving for home, a young man came to the doorway and stood there, smiling. He was much taller and more muscular now, but Mrs. Warren recognized him within seconds. It was Tom! He rushed to her and hugged her so hard her glasses slid down her nose.

"Where have you been?" she said, adjusting her glasses and looking at him intently. My—he was so clear-eyed, so happy and self-confident!

"In school," he said, laughing.

"But I thought—"

"Sure, you thought I was in the navy… Well, I was, for a while. I went to school there."

It was a long story he had to tell. Thanks to the navy he was able to finish high school…and then he went on to college courses. When his enlistment was up, he got a job and continued his education at night. During that time he met a lovely girl. By the time he graduated he was

married and had a son. Then he went on to graduate school, also at night.

"Well, what are you doing with your fine education?" Mrs. Warren asked.

"I'm a teacher—I teach English…especially to kids who disrupt other classes."

Tom had never forgotten the feeling of acceptance he had had from that first day in Mrs. Warren's class. More than all the threats, all the arguments and confrontations he had known, her forgiving love got through to him. And now he was passing that love on to other young people. He had learned the give-and-take of forgiveness.

Do not follow where
the path may lead.
Go instead where
there is no path
and leave a trail.

RALPH WALDO EMERSON

Leadership

Are you a leader?

Look behind and see

if anyone is following.

He who thinks he is leading

And no one is following

Is only taking a walk.

AUTHOR UNKNOWN

Having been a competitive gymnast, I'm a stickler on form. Some time ago I was teaching a class of three- and four-year-olds. I demonstrated a forward roll, explaining every move until the roll was fully executed.

"Now," I said, "I want you to do exactly what I just did. Do you have any questions?"

A wide-eyed youngster timidly raised her hand.

"Miss Michele," she asked, "how do we make our knees crack?"

MICHELE CUNNINGHAM

A Good Lesson

AUTHOR UNKNOWN

RETOLD BY ARTIN TELLALIAN

A young man, a student in one of our universities, was one day taking a walk with a professor, who was commonly called the students' friend, from his kindness to those who waited on his instructions. As they went along, they saw lying in the path a pair of old shoes, which they supposed to belong to a poor man who was employed in a field close by, and who had nearly finished his day's work.

The student turned to the professor, saying: "Let us play the man a trick: we will hide his shoes, and conceal ourselves behind those bushes, and wait to see his perplexity when he cannot find them."

"My young friend," answered the professor, "we should never amuse ourselves at the expense of the poor. But you

are rich, and may give yourself a much greater pleasure by means of this poor man. Put a coin into each shoe, and then we will hide ourselves and watch how the discovery affects him."

The student did so, and they both placed themselves behind the bushes close by. The poor man soon finished his work and came across the field to the path where he had left his coat and shoes. While putting on his coat he slipped his foot into one of his shoes; but feeling something hard, he stooped down to feel what it was and found the coin. Astonishment and wonder were seen upon his countenance. He gazed upon the coin, turned it round, and looked at it again and again. He then looked around him on all sides, but no person was to be seen. He now put the money into his pocket, and proceeded to put on the other shoe; but his surprise was doubled on finding the other coin. His feelings overcame him; he fell upon his knees, looked up to heaven and uttered aloud a

fervent thanksgiving, in which he spoke of his wife, sick and helpless, and his children without bread, whom this timely bounty, from some unknown hand, would save from perishing.

The student stood there deeply affected, and his eyes filled with tears. "Now," said the professor, "are you not much better pleased than if you had played your intended trick?"

The youth replied, "You have taught me a lesson which I will never forget. I feel now the truth of these words, which I never understood before: 'It is more blessed to give than to receive.'"

He that governs well leads the blind;

but he that teaches, gives him eyes.

ROBERT SOUTH

Train a child in the way he should go... And when he is old he will not turn from it.

Proverbs 22:6

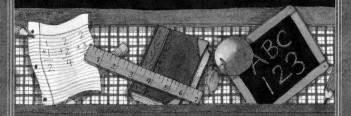

Piece by Piece

Good character is more to be praised

than outstanding talent.

Most talents are, to some extent, a gift.

Good character, by contrast, is not given to us.

We have to build it piece by piece—

By thought, choice, courage and determination.

JOHN LUTHER

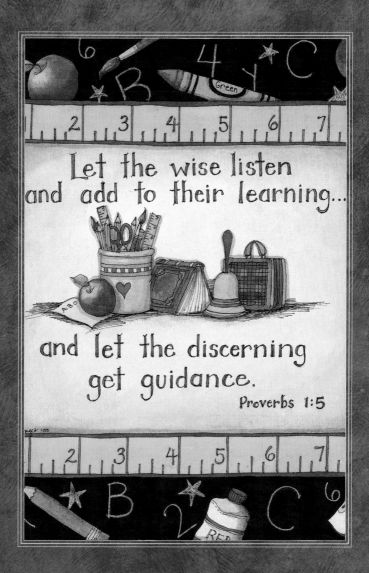

Let the wise listen
and add to their learning...

and let the discerning
get guidance.

Proverbs 1:5

Three Letters from Teddy

ELIZABETH SILANCE BALLARD

Teddy's letter came today and now that I've read it, I will place it in my cedar chest with the other things that are important to life.

"I wanted you to be the first to know."

I smiled as I read the words he had written and my heart swelled with a pride that I had no right to feel.

I have not seen Teddy Stallard since he was a student in my fifth-grade class fifteen years ago. It was early in my career, and I had been teaching for only two years.

From the first day he stepped into my classroom, I disliked Teddy. Teachers (although everyone knows differently) are not supposed to have favorites in a class, but most especially are they not to show dislike for a child…any child.

Nevertheless, every year there are one or two children that one cannot help but be attached to, for teachers are

human, and it is human nature to like bright, pretty, intelligent people, whether they are ten years old or twenty-five. And sometimes, not too often, fortunately, there will be one or two students to whom the teacher just can't seem to relate.

I had thought myself quite capable of handling my personal feelings along that line until Teddy walked into my life. There wasn't a child I particularly liked that year, but Teddy was most assuredly one I disliked.

His physical faults were many—he was often dirty and his hair was unkempt—and his intellect left a lot to be desired. By the end of the first week I knew he was hopelessly behind the others. Not only was he behind; he was just plain slow! I began to withdraw from him.

Any teacher will tell you that it's more of a pleasure to teach a bright child, keeping him challenged and learning, while she puts her major effort on the slower ones. Any teacher can do this. Most teachers do it, but I didn't, not that year.

In fact, I concentrated on my best students and let the others follow along as best they could. Ashamed as I am to admit it, I took pleasure in using my red pen; and each time I came to Teddy's paper, the cross marks were always a little larger and a little redder than necessary.

"Poor work!" I would write with a flourish.

While I did not actually ridicule the boy, my attitude was obviously quite apparent to the class, for he quickly became the class "goat," the outcast.

He knew I didn't like him, but he didn't know why. Nor did I know—then or now—why I felt such a dislike for him. All I know is that he was a little boy no one cared about, and I made no effort on his behalf.

The days rolled by. We made it through the Fall Festival and the Thanksgiving holidays, and I continued marking happily with my red pen. As the Christmas holidays approached, I knew that Teddy would never catch up in time to be promoted to the sixth grade level. He would be a repeater.

To justify myself, I went to his cumulative folder from time to time. He had very low grades for the first four years, but no grade failure. How he had made it, I didn't know. I closed my mind to the personal remarks.

First grade: Teddy shows promise by work and attitude, but has poor home situation. Second grade: Teddy could do better. Mother terminally ill. He received little help at home. Third grade: Teddy is a pleasant boy. Helpful, but too serious. Slow learner. Mother passed away end of the year. Fourth grade: Very slow, but well behaved. Father shows no interest.

Well, they had passed him four times, but "He will certainly repeat fifth grade!" I said to myself.

And then the last day before the holiday arrived. Our little tree on the reading table sported paper and popcorn chains. Many gifts were heaped underneath, waiting for the big moment.

Teachers always get several gifts at Christmas, but mine that year seemed bigger and more elaborate than

ever. There was not a student who had not brought me one. Each unwrapping brought squeals of delight, and the proud giver would receive effusive thank-yous.

His gift wasn't the last one I picked up; in fact it was in the middle of the pile. Its wrapping was a brown paper bag, and he had colored Christmas trees and red bells all over it. It was stuck together with masking tape.

"For Miss Thompson, from Teddy," it read.

The group was completely silent and for the first time I felt conspicuous, embarrassed because they all stood watching me unwrap the gift.

As I removed the last bit of masking tape, two items fell to my desk; a gaudy rhinestone bracelet with several stones missing and a small bottle of dime-store cologne—half empty.

I could hear the snickers and whispers, and I wasn't sure I could look at Teddy.

"Isn't this lovely?" I asked, placing the bracelet on my wrist. "Teddy, would you help me fasten it?"

He smiled shyly as he fixed the clasp, and I held up my wrist for all of them to admire.

There were a few hesitant oohs and ahhs, but as I dabbed the cologne behind my ears, all the little girls lined up for a dab behind their ears.

I continued to open gifts until I reached the bottom of the pile. We ate our refreshments, and the bell rang.

The children filed out with shouts of "See you next year!" and "Merry Christmas!" but Teddy waited at his desk.

When they had all left, he walked up to me, clutching his gift and books to his chest.

"You smell just like my mom," he said softly. "Her bracelet looks real pretty on you too. I'm glad you liked it."

He left quickly. I locked the door, sat down at my desk, and wept, resolving to make up to Teddy what I had deliberately deprived him of—a teacher who cared.

I stayed every afternoon with Teddy from the end of Christmas holidays until the last day of school. Sometimes we worked together. Sometimes he worked alone

while I drew up lesson plans or graded papers.

Slowly but surely he caught up with the rest of the class. In fact, his final averages were among the highest in the class, and although I knew he would be moving out of the state when school was out, I was not worried for him. Teddy had reached a level that would stand him in good stead the following year, no matter where he went. He had enjoyed a measure of success, and as we were taught in our teacher training course, "Success builds success."

I did not hear from Teddy until seven years later, when his first letter appeared in my mailbox.

Dear Miss Thompson,

> *I just wanted you to be the first to know,*
I will be graduating second in my class next month.
Very Truly Yours,
Teddy Stallard

I sent him a card of congratulations and a small package, a pen and pencil gift set. I wondered what he would do after graduation.

Four years later, Teddy's second letter came.

Dear Miss Thompson,

I wanted you to be the first to know. I was just informed that I'll be graduating first in my class. The university has not been easy, but I like it.

Very Truly Yours,
Teddy Stallard

I sent him a good pair of sterling silver monogrammed cuff links and a card, so proud of him I could burst!

And now today—Teddy's third letter.

Dear Miss Thompson,

I wanted you to be the first to know. As of today I am Theodore Stallard, M.D. How about that!!?? I'm going to be married in July, the 27th, to be exact.

I wanted to ask if you could come and sit where Mom would sit if she were here. I'll have no family there as Dad died last year.

Very Truly Yours,
Teddy Stallard

I'm not sure what kind of a gift one sends to a doctor on completion of medical school and state boards. Maybe I'll just wait and take a wedding gift, but a note can't wait.

Dear Ted,

Congratulations! You made it, and you did it yourself! In spite of those like me and not because of us, this day has come for you.

God bless you. I'll be at the wedding with bells on!

A loving, caring teacher

took a liking to me.

She noticed the potential

and helped shape it.

TOM BRADLEY

We will continue to learn

The rest of our lives.

We will learn from our failures

And our successes.

We will learn by growing older,

By suffering, by loving,

By taking risk and by accepting

What we cannot change.

KATHLEEN BRADY

GRADUATION SPEECH

While reviewing math symbols with my second-grade pupils, I drew a greater-than (>) and a less-than (<) sign on the chalkboard and asked, "Does anyone remember what these mean?"

A few moments passed and then a boy confidently raised his hand. "One means fast-forward," he exclaimed, "and the other means rewind!"

TERESA DONN

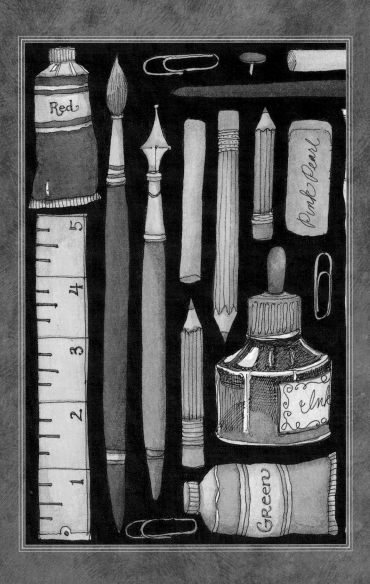

Perceptive?

GARY SMALLEY AND JOHN TRENT

$\mathcal{S}$ixth grade hadn't been a banner year for Eric. Never very confident in school, he had a particular dread of mathematics. "A mental block," one of the school's counselors had told him. Then, as if a mental math block wasn't enough for an eleven-year-old kid to deal with, he came down with measles in the fall and had to stay out of school for two weeks. By the time he got back, his classmates were multiplying fractions. Eric was still trying to figure out what you got when you put a half pie with three-quarters of a pie…besides a lot of pie.

Eric's teacher, Mrs. Gunther—loud, overweight, and terrifying—was unsympathetic. For the rest of the year she hounded him with ceaseless makeup assignments. When his mental block prevented his progress in fractions, she would thunder at him in front of the class,

"I don't care for your excuses! You'd better straighten up!"

The mental block, once the size of a backyard fence, now loomed like the Great Wall of China. Eric despaired of ever catching up, and even fell behind in subjects he'd been good at.

Then came the remarkable moment.

It happened in the middle of Mrs. Warwick's ninth grade English class. To this day, some twenty-five years later, Eric still lights up as he recalls the Moment.

The fifth period class had been yawning through Mrs. Warwick's attempts to spark discussion about a Mark Twain story. At some point in the lecture, something clicked in Eric's mind. It was probably crazy, but it suddenly seemed like he understood something Twain had been driving at—something a little below the surface. Despite himself, Eric raised his hand and ventured an observation.

That led to the moment when Mrs. Warwick looked straight into Eric's eyes, beamed with pleasure, and said,

"Why, Eric…that was *very* perceptive of you!"

Perceptive. Perceptive? Perceptive!

The word echoed in Eric's thoughts for the rest of the day—and then for the rest of his life. *Perceptive? Me? Well, yeah. I guess that WAS perceptive. Maybe I AM perceptive.*

One word, one little positive word dropped at the right moment somehow tipped the balance in a teenager's view of himself—and possibly changed the course of his life, even though he still can't multiply fractions.

Eric went on to pursue a career in journalism and eventually became a book editor, working successfully with some of the top authors in America.

Many teachers are well aware how praise motivates children. One teacher said she praised each student in her third grade class every day, without exception. Her students were the most motivated, encouraged, and enthusiastic in the school. I remember what happened when my high school geometry teacher began to affirm me regularly. Within six weeks my D average climbed to an A.

It's wonderful when a teacher has the opportunity to inject a word of affirmation into a child's life. It's even better when that opportunity is seized. But perhaps the greatest honor of any teacher is seeing a child's eyes light up when they discover something new about themselves and about the world around them. It's what kindles their pride in being called "teacher."

Kind words are the music of the world.

They have power that seems

to be beyond natural causes,

as if they were some angel's song

that had lost its way

and come to earth

FREDRICK WILLIAM FABER

A Teacher Learns a Lesson

CHERYL KIRKING

I was just twenty-two when I landed my first teaching job at a large city high school. Fresh out of college, I was anxious to teach. But I found that I still had a lot of learning to do.

I learned many things in that first year, but my greatest lesson came from John, a tall, gangly sophomore in my fifth-hour American studies class. On the first day of class, John interrupted me frequently with one-liners and complained loudly about how uncomfortable the desks were for his awkward, six-foot-three-inch frame. He wasn't malicious, just pesky; I knew I was going to have to win him over to my side or it would be a long year indeed. I could see that he not only needed a lot of attention, he was needy in other ways as well: His shoes had holes in them, and his clothes were obviously well worn.

The next day I informed John that his new seat was

front row, center, where he could stretch out his legs under the condition that he pull his size-fourteen feet back whenever I needed to walk by.

"Admit it, Miss Kirking, you just want me closer to your desk because I'm your favorite student!" he joked.

"John, you are so smart; you saw right through my little ploy!"

John seemed content with the arrangement, and I could tell that he tried very hard to keep his outbursts to a minimum. Whenever he was too loud or began to interrupt, an admonishing glance was all it took for him to bring his mouth under control. He was usually the first to class, which met right after lunch. He would saunter in, drop his books loudly on his desk, and announce, "Miss Kirking, your favorite student has arrived!"

"Thank you, John," I would reply with a bow, "for gracing us yet another day with your presence!"

Near the end of the first semester, I was having a particularly frustrating day. I had a terrible head cold

and was grumpy and tired. The students were complaining about the upcoming final exam, and I was having trouble getting them to settle down. When I finally got everyone's attention, I warned the students, "I am passing out your assignment. I want you to get to work immediately and be quiet—and I don't want to hear one more word!"

"How about two more words?" John quipped.

"John," I snapped, "shut up!" John winced as if I had slapped him. The hurt and embarrassment in his eyes made me immediately regret my harsh words.

I was so ashamed. I had been raised not to use the words "shut up." I couldn't blame it on the unruly students or my head cold or John. I had blown it—and it was my responsibility to fix it somehow. How could I have been so disrespectful? As the sullen students worked silently on their assignments, I wondered what I should do. I feared I had broken the trust that John and I had established.

"John," I said, loudly enough for the rest of the class

to hear, "I didn't show you much respect today. I am really sorry."

Still looking stunned, John shrugged and answered softly, "It's okay."

Finally the bell rang, and the class shuffled out. John lingered behind and slowly approached my desk.

"I can't believe you said that to me," he remarked incredulously.

"I know, John, I shouldn't have told you to shut up."

"No," he replied, "not that you told me to shut up. I can't believe that you said you were sorry. That's pretty cool." He gave me a little smile as he turned to leave.

John helped me learn one of my most important lessons as an educator: Respect and kindness are my most powerful tools.

Instruction does not prevent

wasted time or mistakes;

and mistakes themselves are

often the best teachers of all.

JAMES A. FROUDE

Wanted

More to improve and fewer to disapprove.

More doers and fewer talkers.

More to say it can be done

And fewer to say it's impossible.

More to inspire others

And fewer to throw cold water on them.

More to get into the thick of things

And fewer to sit on the sidelines.

More to point out what's right

And fewer to show what's wrong.

More to light a candle

And fewer to curse the darkness.

AUTHOR UNKNOWN

To Gilbert

CAROL W. MARDIROSSIAN

Gilbert was the worst student that crossed my path that first day of school. He came in with no book, pencil, or even paper. He slept through the first thirty minutes until finally I stood directly over him to keep him awake. After class, I kept him for a motivational speech. It was to be one of many with this unruly youngster. After my verbal lashing, he simply said, "Miss Walker, I like you fine. It's just that English ain't never been my thing. I think it's boring and a waste of time. I figure it's a good chance to get a nap before gym. I need my rest to play good."

Shaking my head, I searched for something inspiring to say. Poetic, inspirational messages danced in my head, and then finally I said, "Well, Gilbert. I'll give you a good reason to pay attention in my class. You're never going to graduate if you don't, and I'm going to write you up every

day that you breathe hard." I exhaled and grabbed my throbbing head.

Day in and day out for the entire first semester Gilbert came in and enjoyed his rest before gym class. I did as I promised and wrote him up every now and then, to no avail. I gave him extra homework that he didn't do and kept him for detentions. Of course he never showed up. I even wrote his name on the board followed by a long succession of checks. Nothing seemed to work with him.

One day the light came on. I decided that we would have a class spelling bee. My department head had originally asked me to choose the best spellers from my college prep class to participate in the school spelling bee. It was assumed that no one from Gilbert's class would even be in the running. I thought, however, that they should all enjoy the chance. Something magical happened as Gilbert continually spelled words correctly throughout the entire proceeding. It finally came down to

the smartest and prettiest little girl in the room and Gilbert, standing there in his faded jeans and ragged T-shirt. I called out the most difficult word of the contest yet, and the little girl answered incorrectly. I looked at Gilbert and he looked at me with panic. I prayed over and over in my mind, *Please, God, let him get it right.* He started to spell the word. He did so slowly and hesitantly. I couldn't stand it. Finally, the moment came and I pronounced him the winner. The whole class cheered as he strutted across the front of the room.

I told the department head that Gilbert would be in the school spelling bee. She couldn't believe it but accepted the news with grace. Of course, Gilbert didn't win the school spelling bee, but that didn't matter. He was there. His mother came to watch and had even bought him a new suit of clothes to wear for the special occasion. Pictures were taken by his mother; and for the day, Gilbert was someone special. The truth is he was all along.

Gilbert never slept in class again. Instead, he began

talking incessantly throughout every lesson that I attempted. Somehow it didn't bother me as much anymore. Every now and then he would complete a homework assignment or actually pass a test. I argued with him at times as if I were a child myself competing for attention. There were days when every nerve I had was worn down by him.

The last day of school came. As the bell rang, all of the children ran from the room including Gilbert. I sighed a huge sigh of relief and sat at my desk for a moment to enjoy the silence. Catching my attention from a glance was a little sheet of notebook paper torn off and folded over. It said on the front, "To Miss Walker."

The inside message simply read, "I have enjoyed being in your room this year. I think I even learned a thing or two."

After a refreshing summer, I returned for another year. I walked into my classroom to get ready for the day and there, already seated, was Gilbert. He said, "I'm gonna be in your class again. I asked the assistant principal if I could and she said yes."

I adorned a fake smile and said, "Oh, that's great." The new year proceeded much like the last with a long string of warnings and detentions, mostly for talking. At least he wasn't sleeping in class.

With each new day our relationship as teacher and student grew into one of mutual respect and friendship. Every time he did something bad he gave me his sly little grin, and I just couldn't bring myself to be harsh with him. Instead, I stayed after school tutoring him and helping him pass my class and his other classes.

Near the end of the year, I became engaged and knew that I was going to be moving to a new town. Gilbert came every day of post-planning to help me pack up all of my belongings to begin another life far away.

He said on our last day together, "You're the greatest teacher I've ever had. I probably won't ever like English again because nobody does it as good as you do." I gave him another one of my motivational speeches, except this time I spoke from my heart. I encouraged him to go

on and do great things. I knew he was capable of so much.

Every year since, I began the school year saying to myself, "Well, who is going to be my Gilbert this year?" I would laugh and always go on to meet his replacement.

Eight years after leaving Gilbert's school, I talked to one of the teachers. My first question was, "What ever happened to Gilbert?"

She began by saying, "Well, he never liked English again, but he did pretty well in school. He had some hard times, though, because he couldn't break himself away from some of his friends that were drinking and doing drugs." After a long pause, she continued and revealed to me that Gilbert had died in a wreck just a few weeks before he could graduate. His pregnant girlfriend was in the car with him, but, fortunately, she and the baby were fine. The child was born and named after him.

The news shook me terribly. I wonder if Gilbert knows that he touched my life more than I touched his. He taught me that even the most unlovable child is worth

loving. With such a great age and cultural difference, we had become friends. On my next year of teaching I started a new tradition. Instead of wondering who my next Gilbert would be, I spent those few seconds in prayer before any of the students arrived. I asked God to help me love all of my students and to teach at least one person one thing. I held my hand in the air as if toasting and said aloud, "To Gilbert."

The true aim of everyone who
aspires to be a teacher should be,
not to impart his own opinions,
but to kindle minds.

FREDERICK WILLIAM ROBERTSON

We Could Have Danced All Night

GUY RICE DOUD

*A*s adviser to our high school student council I worked with the leadership to encourage projects that involved student service. I was impressed with my students' enthusiasm for helping with local canned-food drives and other events to aid charity.

Our "Adopt-a-Grandparent" program had been rewarding for the students who had been involved. They had grown as people by discovering the worth of others. I believe that the true leader is the true servant, and I tried to convey that message to my students. But it never got through to them as clearly as it did the night of the prom.

Tom Rosenberger had given me a call. A friend, and one of the local elementary principals, Tom had heard of an idea at a conference he had attended and called to

share the idea with me. I fell in love with it and soon shared it with my student council.

"Mr. President?" I asked.

Mike, the president of the student council, acknowledged me. "Yes, Mr. Doud?"

I started gradually. "I've been thinking of an idea, and I want to bounce it off everyone."

"What's the idea?" asked Mike.

"I think we should host a prom," I said.

"We already have a prom!" answered about thirty students all at once, who seemed to wonder if I had lost my mind. They knew that organizing the prom was the responsibility of the junior class cabinet.

"Oh, I don't mean a prom for eleventh and twelfth graders," I said.

"We're not going to include sophomores!" said one senior boy.

"No. I want to have a prom for senior—" but they didn't let me finish.

"Seniors can already go to the prom," Mike answered, wondering what had gone wrong with his adviser.

"No, for senior citizens. People fifty-five years of age and over. Let's hold a prom for them."

"Why would we want to do that?" asked Mike.

"Let's take the money we've earned this year," I said, "and let's give it back to the community in the form of a gift. That gift will be a prom. We'll invite all senior citizens to come. We'll decorate the gym, hire an orchestra, have corsages for the ladies…." I was beginning to show some real excitement.

"If we spent money doing that, does that mean we wouldn't take our usual spring trip?" asked one girl, putting down the mirror she held in her hand.

"We would spend as much of the money as necessary to make this a most special evening for the senior citizens. The orchestra we hire will play the big band sounds of the twenties and thirties and other dance music. I've already contacted an orchestra, and I've talked with our principal,

who thinks it's a great idea. I told him that I thought you guys would think it's a great idea, too." I can be pretty persuasive sometimes.

After much discussion, the council voted to form a committee to plan the senior citizen prom. In the weeks to follow, I watched my students become excited about the prom. Some of the young men in the council decided to order tuxedos so they would look nice as hosts. The girls planned to wear their long dresses to serve as hostesses.

All of Brainerd got excited the week before the prom. Paul Harvey began page two of his national daily broadcast this way: "In Brainerd, Minnesota, the student council is planning a prom...for senior citizens. That's right! A prom...for senior citizens. The Brainerd students are going to provide an orchestra, corsages, valet parking, free hors d'oeuvres and...they are also going to do the chaperoning!"

I had been somewhat concerned about the lack of advertising. My students had contacted the senior citizen

centers in the area and had sent out invitations, but when I heard it announced by Paul Harvey, my fears of poor publicity died.

The night of the prom finally arrived. The students had decorated our gym more beautifully than I had ever seen it. It was like the gym I had seen in my dreams when I had been in high school. The floral department at the vocational school had donated corsages, some of the local banks provided the hors d'oeuvres, the bus company that contracts with the school district provided free transportation to any senior citizen needing it. My students had tried to cover all the bases. We sat back to wait and see how many seniors would attend. The prom was to begin at six-thirty. At four o'clock, they started to come!

One of the first to arrive was an older lady with a cane. She stopped inside the door and looked around.

"Oh," she said, "so this is the new high school."

I didn't remind her that the high school was more than fifteen years old.

"I've never been in here before," she said.

Mark Dinham, one of the main organizers of the prom, grabbed a corsage and asked her if he could pin it on her. She readily agreed.

"The prom doesn't begin until six-thirty," Mark said.

"I'll wait," she said. "I want to get a good seat."

"I hope you'll do some dancing!" I said.

"I'll dance if you dance with me!" she replied as Mark finished pinning her corsage.

He turned a bit red. "Sure, I'll dance with you, but I've got to go home and change clothes," he said.

A few moments later, a couple walked up to the table. "Is this where the prom is being held?" they asked.

"That's right," I said.

I could hardly believe what they had to say: "We're from Oregon, and we're on our way to Wisconsin. We heard it on Paul Harvey yesterday, so we looked up Brainerd on the map and decided to go a little out of our way so we could come to your prom. Are we welcome?"

And people kept coming. By 6:30 when the prom began, more than five hundred senior citizens packed the transformed gymnasium.

But we had developed one major problem. Mike was the first to call it to my attention. I had noticed him dancing with one lady after another. He wasn't able to take a break.

"Mr. Doud," he said, "we have a serious male shortage here."

"What are you going to do about it, Mike?" I asked.

"I know where some of the hockey team is tonight, and I think I could call them and tell them to go home and get their suits on and get over here."

"Good plan," I said.

Soon some of Mike's friends started to arrive. I watched as the lady who had been the first to come walked up to one of the sophomores who had just entered the gym.

"You come dance with me," she said, grabbing his hand before he was sure what had happened.

Mike came up to me. "This is fun. Where did they learn to dance like this?"

Mike and many of my students were amazed that some dances actually had set steps and patterns. I joined in as the senior citizens taught us to waltz and polka. I had never learned to dance, either.

One of the seniors who had dressed up for the occasion had on a beautiful long dress with sequins, and the mirrored ball in the middle of the dance floor reflected light off her dress. We danced. She led.

"If I were about sixty years younger, I'd go after you," she said.

I laughed.

"What grade are you in?" she asked.

I laughed harder. "I'm a teacher here. I'm in charge of these kids."

"Oh," she said, "you're so young and handsome."

I didn't laugh. "And you are very beautiful," I said.

"Oh, come on now...."

The orchestra began to play a song from *My Fair Lady*, and as I followed my partner, I thought of Eliza Doolittle. Henry Higgins saw an elegant woman when everyone else saw a peasant.

"I could have danced all night...." My partner sang along with the music. "That was a good movie," she added, "but I bet it's before your time."

"No, I remember it well." I looked about at my students, every one of them dancing with a senior citizen.

One older man was teaching a sophomore girl how to waltz. I watched her. I was used to seeing her in torn blue jeans. She was beautiful in a long dress.

When the evening finally came to an end, no one wanted to leave.

Mike walked up to me. "That was the most fun I've ever had in high school."

"You mean that was more fun than your junior-senior proms?" I asked.

"No question about it." Mike was definite.

"What made this so much fun?" I asked.

Without thinking for even a moment, Mike answered, "It really feels good to do something for somebody else."

The following Monday, Paul Harvey, who must have spies all about, concluded his broadcast with this story: "Remember last week I told you about how the Brainerd, Minnesota, student council was going to host a prom for senior citizens? Well, they did…and more than five hundred senior citizens showed up. The high school students danced with the seniors, and the chaperons report no major problems…. Oh, there was a little smooching in the corner, but no major problems."

"Paul Harvey, good day!"

A wisely chosen illustration is
almost essential to fasten the truth
upon the ordinary mind, and
no teacher can afford to neglect
this part of his preparation.

HOWARD CROSBY

Life 101

PHIL CALLAWAY

I'm learning that some of the most successful people I know didn't have a clue what the future held on graduation day.

I'm learning that a good sense of humor is money in the bank. In life. On the job. In a marriage.

I'm learning that a good attitude can control situations you can't. That any bad experience can be a good one. It all depends on me.

I'm learning that you can do something in an instant that will give you heartache for life.

I'm learning that bitterness and gossip accomplish nothing, but forgiveness and love accomplish everything.

I'm learning that it takes years to build trust, and seconds to destroy it.

I'm learning to always leave loved ones with loving words. It may be the last time I see them.

I'm learning that if I'm standing on the edge of a cliff, the best way forward is to back up. That you don't fail when you lose, you fail when you quit.

I'm learning that too many people spend a lifetime stealing time from those who love them the most. Trying to please the ones who care about them the least.

I'm learning that money is a lousy way of keeping score. That true success is not measured in cars, or homes, or bank accounts, but in relationships. Put God first. The others will follow.

I'm learning that having enough money isn't nearly as much fun as I thought it would be when I didn't have any. That money buys less that you think. A house but not a home. Vacations but not peace. Sex but not love.

I'm learning that helping others is far more rewarding than helping myself. That those who laugh more worry less. That when I grow up I wanna be a kid.

I'm learning that you cannot make anyone love you. But you can work on being loveable.

I'm learning that I will never regret a moment spent reading the Bible or praying. Or a kind word. Or a day at the beach.

I'm learning that laughter and tears are nothing to be ashamed of. To celebrate the good things. And pray about the bad.

And I'm learning that the most important thing in the world is loving God. That everything good comes from that.

If we work upon brass,

time will efface it;

If we rear temples,

they will crumble into dust;

But if we work

upon immortal souls,

If we imbue them with principles,

With the just fear of the creator and

love of fellow men,

We engrave on those tablets

something which will

brighten all eternity.

DANIEL WEBSTER

If we don't model what we teach,

we are teaching something else.

AUTHOR UNKNOWN

Acknowledgments

A diligent search has been made to trace original ownership, and when necessary, permission to reprint has been obtained. If I have overlooked giving proper credit to anyone, please accept my apologies. Should any attribution be found to be incorrect, the publisher welcomes written documentation supporting correction for subsequent printings. For material not in the public domain, grateful acknowledgment is given to the publishers and individuals who have granted permission for use of their material. Acknowledgments are listed by story title in the order they appear in the book. For permission to reprint any of the stories, please request permission from the original source listed below.

"The Student's Mite" by David R. Collins © 1986. Used by permission of the author.

"Hope Which Springs Eternal" from *Molder of Dreams* by Guy Rice Doud, a Focus on the Family book published by Tyndale House. Copyright © 1990 by Guy Doud. All rights reserved. International copyright secured. Used by permission.

Evans and Laura Hobe. Used by permission of Doubleday, a division of Random House, Inc.

Text by Michele Cunningham reprinted with permission from the November 1984 *Reader's Digest*. Copyright © 1984 by The Reader's Digest Assn., Inc.

"A Good Lesson" retold by Artin Tellalian. First published in 1916 by W. & R. Chambers, Ltd., of Great Britain. Used by permission of Artin Tellalian.

"Three Letters from Teddy" by Elizabeth Silance Ballard © 1976. Used by permission of the author.

Quote by Kathleen Brady © 2000. Used by permission of the author.

Text by Teresa Donn reprinted with permission from the February 1990 *Reader's Digest*. Copyright © 1990 by The Reader's Digest Assn., Inc.

"Perceptive?" by Gary Smalley and John Trent from *Leaving the Light On* © 1994. Used by permission of Multnomah Publishers, Sisters, Oregon.

"A Teacher Learns a Lesson" by Cheryl Kirking taken from *Ripples of Joy* by Cheryl Kirking. Used by permission of WaterBrook Press.